FUN FACTS

For Five Year Olds

This book belongs to ....

Contents

Page 1: Amazing Animals

Page 3: Dino Time

Page 5: Our Awesome Bodies

Page 7: Wacky Weather

Page 9: Super Space

Page 11: Brilliant Bugs

Page 13: Yummy in my Tummy

Page 15: Around the World

Page 17: Back in the Olden Days

Page 19: Random Facts

Page 21: Quiz Time

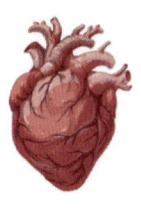

Amazing Animals

A giraffe's tongue is so long it can lick its own ears! Also, giraffes only have 7 bones in their necks — the same number as humans!

Kangaroos can't walk backwards because their tails are too big and strong.

Bats have belly buttons — just like humans!

Sea otters hold hands while they sleep so they don't float away.

Alaskan wood frogs can freeze in winter and hop again in spring! Frogs are also carnivores, which means they only eat meat.

A baby octopus is the size of a flea!

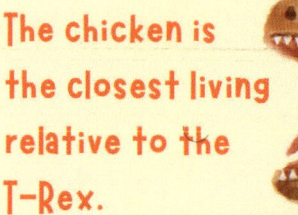

The chicken is the closest living relative to the T-Rex.

People think dogs are totally colour-blind, but really it's just reds and greens that look brown to them. They can see yellows and blues just as well as you can!

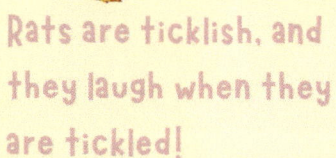

Rats are ticklish, and they laugh when they are tickled!

All cows have different patterns and they can sleep standing up.

Male seahorses are the ones who are pregnant and give birth, not the females.

Horseshoe crabs have blue blood!

Owls can turn their heads nearly all the way around, but they can't move their eyes. This is because their eyes are tube-shaped, not round like ours.

A snail can sleep for 3 years at a time! They also have 20,000 (twenty thousand) teeth!

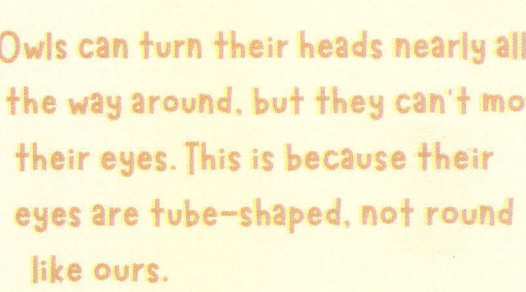

Elephants use their trunks like a snorkel when they swim. They are the largest mammals on land and the only mammals that can't jump!

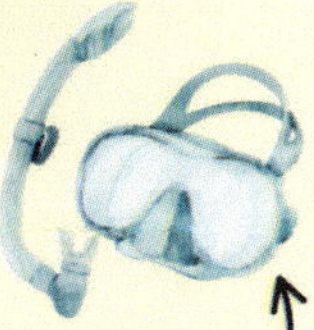

snorkel

Female lions do most of the hunting. You can hear a lion roar 5 miles away!

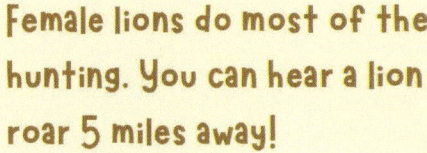

Koalas spend up to 22 hours a day sleeping. (There are only 24 hours in the whole day!)

Dino Time!

The word "dinosaur" means "terrible lizard."

Dinosaurs laid eggs — some were bigger than footballs.

The Microraptor dinosaur was as small as a mouse!

Brachiosaurus was as tall as a four-storey building (about 12-15 metres tall.)

Some dinosaurs had feathers, just like birds.

Most dinosaurs became extinct 65 million years ago. Our world was hit by a huge asteroid, which changed the environment and killed much of the life on Earth.

The Hadrosaur (Had-ruh-saw) had nearly 1,000 teeth — 960 to be exact.

Some dinosaurs lived to be almost 300 years old.

There were more than 700 different types of dinosaurs.

3

The first dinosaur to be formally named was the Megalosaurus (meh-guh-luh-saw-rus).

Dinosaurs often walked together in large groups.

Some of the biggest dinosaurs only ate plants. Animals that only eat plants are called herbivores.

Dinosaur fossils have been found all over the world — even at the South Pole!

Pterodactyls (te-ruh-dak-tls) were flying reptiles. Dinosaurs were non-flying reptiles.

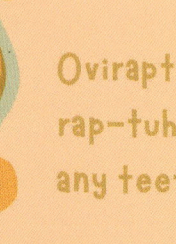

Oviraptors (ow-vuh-rap-tuh) didn't have any teeth!

Dinosaurs lived on Earth for about 165 million years!

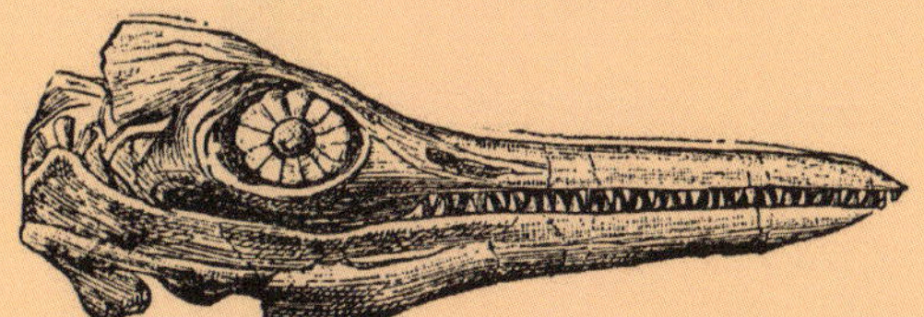

Dinosaurs and humans did NOT live at the same time.

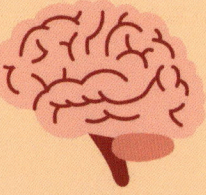

Dinosaurs had small brains compared to their size. They were about as smart as a snake or a lizard.

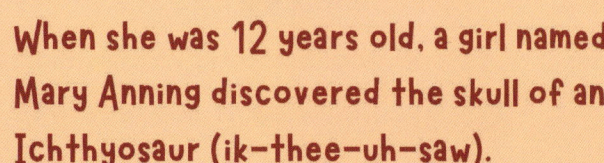

When she was 12 years old, a girl named Mary Anning discovered the skull of an Ichthyosaur (ik-thee-uh-saw).

4

Our Awesome Bodies

In humans, a yawn typically lasts around six seconds. Did you know that animals yawn too?

Your skin is your body's biggest organ. It protects our insides and keeps us the right temperature too.

Human teeth are just as strong as shark teeth.

When you are born, you have 270 bones. As you get older, some of these bones fuse together, and as an adult you will only have 206 bones.

People think that your nose and ears keep growing even when you're an adult. What actually happens is they just get saggy and look bigger.

Over their lifetime, most people spend about 1 whole year sitting on the toilet.

You grow taller when you sleep. If you don't get enough sleep, it makes it harder to remember things.

Babies don't cry any real tears until they are about 1 month old.

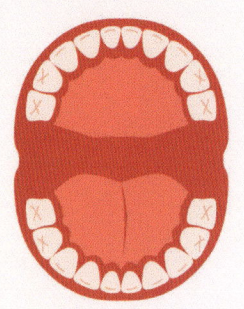 Children have 20 teeth, but when you are an adult, you will have 32.

 All humans fart! On average, you fart enough in one day to fill a party balloon.

More than half of all your bones are in your hands and feet! Did you know that nobody has the same fingerprints or toeprints as anyone else?

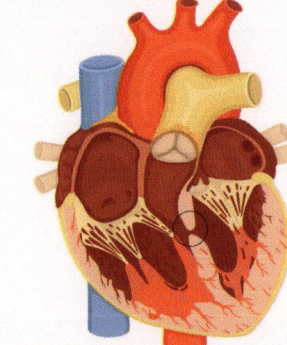 A human heart can actually beat outside the body!

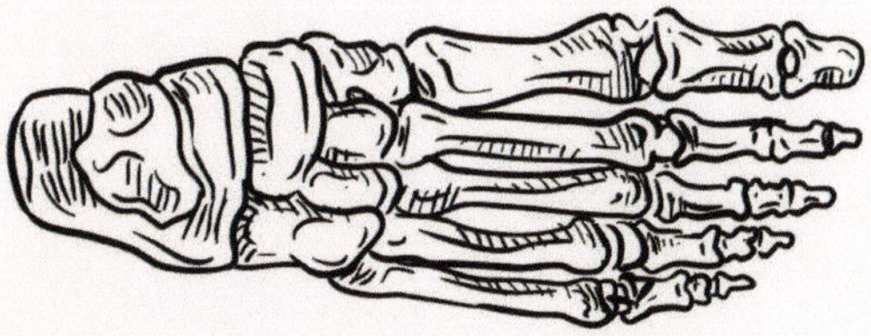

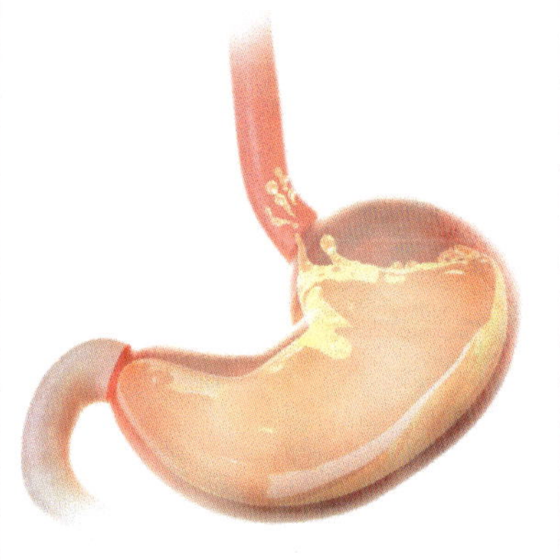

Your brain isn't fully formed until you are 25 years old.

Your stomach makes acid to digest food. It's so strong it can dissolve metal! (Don't try this at home!)

Your biggest muscle in the body is your bottom —the gluteus maximus.

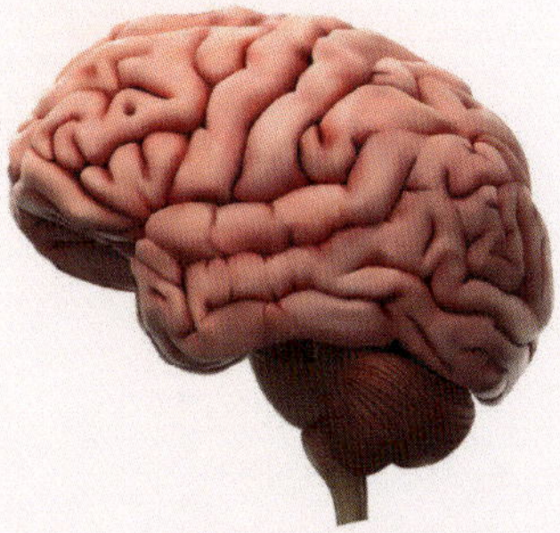

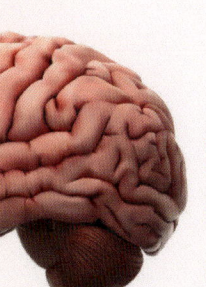 Your brain shrinks if you don't drink enough water, and this can cause headaches.

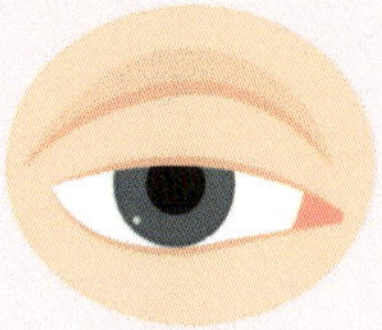

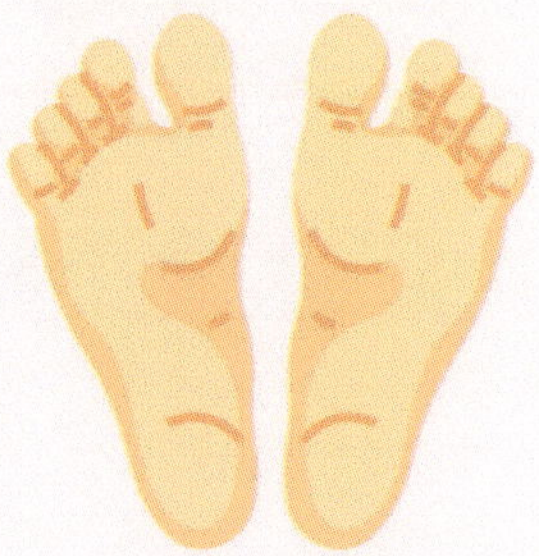

Your brain uses more energy than all of your other organs.

The thickest skin on your body is on your feet, and the thinnest is on your eyelids.

6

Wacky Weather

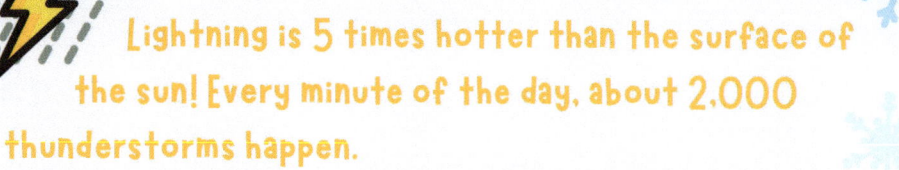

Lightning is 5 times hotter than the surface of the sun! Every minute of the day, about 2,000 thunderstorms happen.

Sometimes the weather is so hot it can make train tracks bend!

All snowflakes have six sides and they are all different!

Rainbows appear when the sun shines through raindrops. You can also get a moonbow when moonlight shines through raindrops!

Clouds are made from a mixture of dry air, liquid water droplets, and ice particles.

In 1684, it was so cold in England that the River Thames froze solid for two months.

When clouds are very low, we call them fog.

The South Pole is actually a desert because it hardly ever rains there!

Raindrops are actually round like little balls, not tear-drop shaped.

The middle of a hurricane is called the eye.

Hurricanes are giant storms that start over the ocean. They spin one way in the Northern Hemisphere and the other way in the Southern Hemisphere.

Worms wriggle up from underground when a flood is coming.

Wildfires sometimes create tornadoes made of fire called fire whirls.

Cape Farewell in Greenland is the windiest place on the planet.

 Some frogs get noisier just before it rains.

8

Super Space

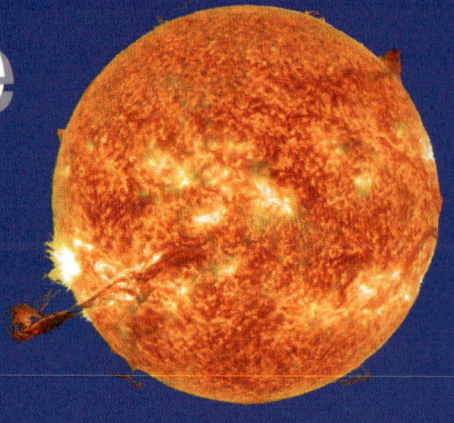

If you could take a rocket to the dwarf planet Pluto, it would take nearly 10 years travelling at 27,000 miles per hour. If you travelled at the speed of an aeroplane, it would take around 600 years.

Over one million Earths could fit inside the sun — 1.3 million to be exact!

The sun is the closest star to Earth and is made of burning gases.

Shooting stars aren't actually stars; they are pieces of rock that burn up when coming towards Earth.

A day on Venus is longer than a year on Venus! This is because it takes longer to spin once than it does to travel all the way around the sun.

The planets Jupiter, Saturn, Uranus, and Neptune are all made of gas! So even if we could visit them, we wouldn't have any ground to walk on!

Did you know that the rings around Saturn are made of ice and rock?

The sunset on Mars looks blue.

You can't talk on the Moon because there is no air to carry sound. This also means we can't hear anything coming from space. If we could, we would be able to hear the Sun!

On 20th July 1969, Neil Armstrong became the first person in history to set foot on the Moon.

Footprints on the Moon don't disappear because there is no wind or rain to wash them away.

The Moon doesn't make its own light; it just reflects light from the Sun.

Uranus is the only planet in our solar system that spins on its side. Venus is the only planet that spins backwards compared to the others.

Astronauts have to take their own oxygen to space so they can breathe.

Brilliant Bugs

Ants can carry things 50 times heavier than their own body weight.

Butterflies taste with their feet, and their wings are made of tiny scales.

Butterflies can see many more colours than humans can.

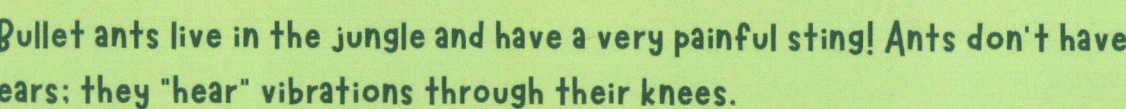

Bullet ants live in the jungle and have a very painful sting! Ants don't have ears; they "hear" vibrations through their knees.

This picture shows a spicebush swallowtail caterpillar.

Some caterpillars have patterns that make them look like snakes.

Caterpillars have about 4,000 muscles. Humans have 600 muscles.

Caterpillars have 12 eyes, but they can't see very well.

Cockroaches can live up to a week without their heads.

Grasshoppers existed before dinosaurs! They make their chirping noise using their wings.

Ladybirds sometimes play dead to avoid being eaten.

Mosquitoes like the smell of smelly human feet. So if you don't want to get bitten by one, wash your feet!

Grasshoppers can jump 20 times the length of their body!

Ladybirds let out a yellow liquid if they think they are in danger. Don't worry though, it isn't wee.

All insects have six legs, and there are over a million different types of insects.

Dragonflies can fly backwards!

In some parts of the world, small spiders are thrown as confetti at weddings.

Bugs can fart!

Spiders aren't insects because they have eight legs! They are called arachnids (ah-rak-nids).

Some insects, like water boatmen, can walk on water!

Yummy in my Tummy

Over a hundred years ago, if you a stomach ache, the doctor might give you ketchup as medicine!

Carrots were originally purple, not orange.

Rhubarb grows so quickly that you can hear it growing!

Bananas are actually a type of berry. One banana is called a finger, and a bunch is called a hand. Monkeys peel bananas upside down compared to humans.

Cheese is the most stolen food in the world (by humans!).

In Colombia, some people eat roasted ants at the cinema instead of popcorn.

Cucumbers are mostly made of water—95% to be exact!

Strawberries are part of the rose family. Did you know they are not actually berries?

M&Ms are named after their creators: Mars and Murrie.

In ancient times, the Aztecs and the Mayans used cacao beans as money. Now we use them to make chocolate.

Ice lollies were invented accidentally by an 11-year-old child called Frank Epperson.

Honey never goes off.

You can test if an egg has gone off by seeing if it floats. If it is okay to eat, it will sink; if it has gone off, it will float. Test this with raw eggs, not cooked eggs!

McDonald's sells over 6 million burgers a day!

Margherita pizza is named after Queen Margherita, who loved cheesy pizza.

Coffee was discovered by a goat herder in Ethiopia (which is in Africa) over 1,000 years ago.

14

Around the World

Egypt

Sudan

Egypt is famous for ancient pyramids, but there are actually more pyramids in Sudan than in Egypt. Sudan is also in Africa, just below Egypt.

The Amazon rainforest produces 20% of all the oxygen that we breathe, which is why we must protect it!

No country officially owns Antarctica.

The world's longest flight lasts 19 hours. It is from Singapore to New York.

The Arctic Ocean is the smallest ocean and is mostly covered by ice.

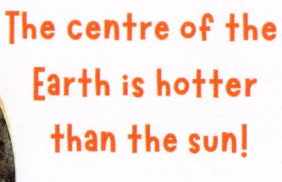
The centre of the Earth is hotter than the sun!

The tallest tree in the world lives in California, North America. It is a coast redwood.

Did you know that some volcanoes are actually underwater in the ocean?

15

Yuma, a city in Arizona (in North America) is the sunniest place in the world.

The shortest name for a town is just one letter. In Sweden, there is a village named Ö, which means "island." In France there is a village called Y.

Canada has more lakes than anywhere else in the world.

Nearly three-quarters of the Earth's surface is covered by water — 71% to be exact.

Hamburg in Germany has the most bridges of any city, with more than 2,500 bridges.

Death Valley in California is where the hottest temperature on Earth was recorded: 56.7°C!

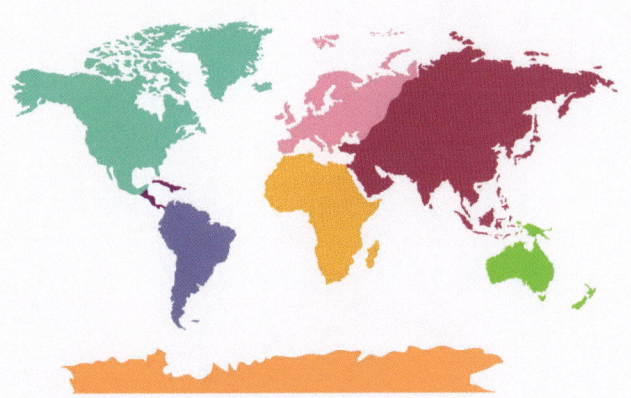

There are officially 195 countries in the world.

There is a place where it rains fish every year! In Honduras, fish are blown out of the ocean and rain down from the sky on to the land. This has been happening for over 100 years.

16

Back in the Olden Days

Tug-of-war was once an Olympic sport.

In ancient Egypt, men and women wore make-up. They believed it had magical healing powers.

The Great Pyramid of Giza in Egypt was the tallest man-made structure for over 3,800 years. Now the tallest structure is the Burj Khalifa in Dubai.

Forks have only been used for a few hundred years. Before that, people speared their food on knives and used a spoon to help.

When tea first came to the UK, it was so expensive that people used to lock it away!

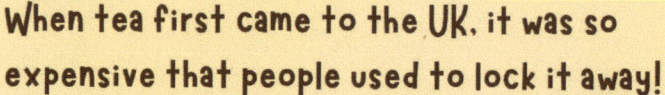

Numbers were invented in India!

The Romans used to poop together! They had big toilet rooms where they could poo and chat.

17

Children used to have jobs in factories, sweeping chimneys or working in the sewers!

The shortest war in history lasted less than 45 minutes. It was between Britain and Zanzibar. Britain won this war and these two countries never fought again.

China invented the lottery and used to send the results by carrier pigeons.

In the 1800s, people used to say "prunes" instead of "cheese" when having their photo taken. They didn't want big smiles in photographs; they were supposed to look serious.

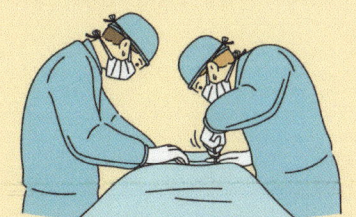

In Victorian times they used to do operations without putting people to sleep because anaesthetic hadn't been invented yet! Ouch!

People used to perform naked at the Olympics! Gymnastics actually comes from the Greek words for athlete and naked.

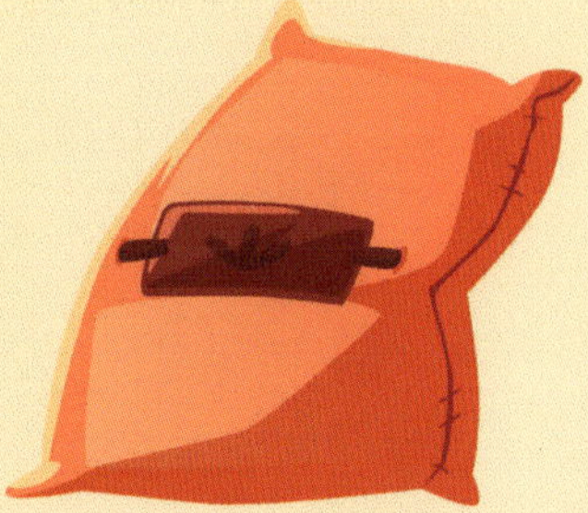

About 100 years ago (1920s), people who didn't have much money made clothes from big food sacks. Because of this, the sack makers started making them more colourful so people could look more fashionable.

18

Random Facts

Dogs can hear high notes that we can't hear!

Camels store fat in their humps, not water.

Peanuts are not actually nuts!

The Eiffel Tower is taller in summer and smaller in winter. It is 15 cm taller when the weather is hotter.

The opposite sides of dice always add up to seven.

A tomato is a fruit, not a vegetable.

Human blood is as salty as the ocean.

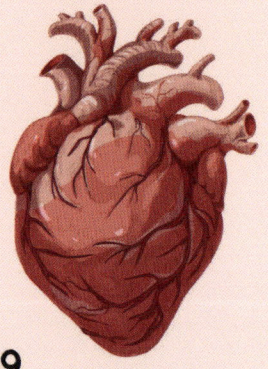

Every minute, all the blood in your body goes through your heart. The blood is pumped to the lungs to collect oxygen, then pumped all over the body to deliver the oxygen.

19

All humans dream, but most dreams are forgotten very quickly after we wake up. Some animals dream too!

The Olympics have been cancelled three times: in 1916, 1940, and 1944. This was because of World War I and World War II.

Even though you can smell when you are asleep, your brain doesn't tell you about it. This is one reason why fire alarms are important. If you smell burning when you're asleep, your brain won't wake you up!

It is impossible to fold a piece of A4 paper in half more than eight times.

Weird laws that still exist in the UK:
It is illegal to draw on money.
It is illegal to fly a kite in the street.
It is also illegal to be annoying in a library.

Your eyes always have a thin layer of tears over the front of them. If it wasn't there, the clear layer at the front of each eye would dry out and go cloudy, and we wouldn't be able to see!

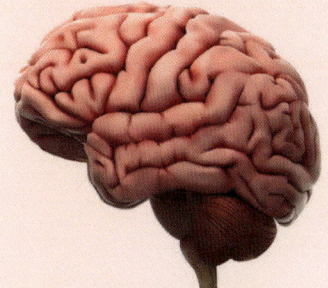

Your brain can't feel pain, so a surgeon can operate on it while you are awake.

In Thailand, kite flying is a sport.

It is impossible to tickle yourself!

20

QUIZ TIME

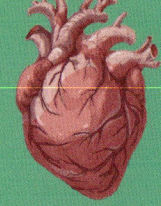

Test yourself and see what you can remember. You can find all of the answers in this book!

1. Is human blood salty or sweet?

2. How long did the shortest war last?

3. Which country invented numbers?

4. What part of their body do butterflies taste with?

5. Which planet spins on its side?

6. What is the most stolen food in the world?

7. Did humans live at the same time as dinosaurs?

8. Which country invented the lottery?

9. Which creature comes out of the ground before a flood?

10. Which city in the world has the most bridges?

11. What was ketchup used as in the past?

12. What did the Victorians say when they had their photo taken?

13. Which is hotter, the centre of the Earth or the sun?

14. How many teeth do children have?

15. Which part of your body has the thinnest skin?

16. How many bones do giraffes have in their neck?

17. What animal can sleep for 22 hours a day?

18. Which animal can freeze in winter and hop again in spring?

19. What is the longest river in the world?

20. Name an animal that can't walk backwards.

More books by Stephanie Lipsey-Liu

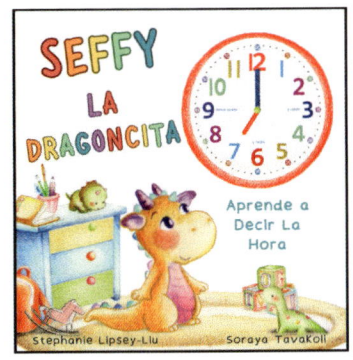
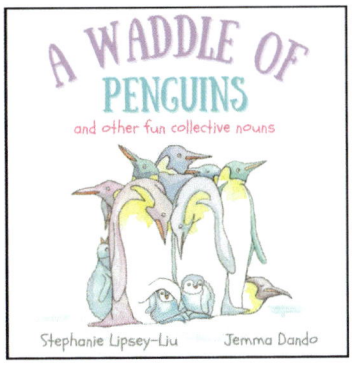
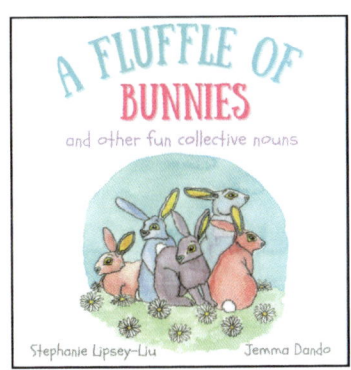
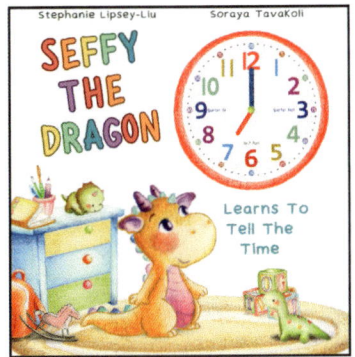

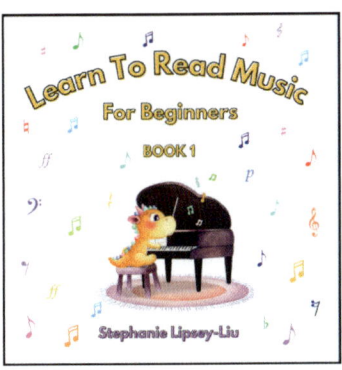

This book is Copyright © 2024 by Stephanie Lipsey-Liu.
All rights reserved

No part of this publication may be reproduced or transmitted in any form or by any means, electronic or mechanical, including photocopying, recording, scanning or otherwise, or through any information browsing, storage or retrieval system, without permission in writing from the publisher.

First printed 2025 ISBN 978-1-917565-02-8

Little Lion Publishing UK

Nottingham, England

www.littlelionpublishing.co.uk

Printed in Dunstable, United Kingdom